# THIS PLANNER BELONGS TO

........................................................................................................................................

........................................................................................................................................

**Self Success Press**

# Social Media Planner

## How to Use This Planner
This Social Media Planner is simply a tool to help you plan and schedule your Social Media Posts. Here are a few things to think about before creating Social Media content:

## Your Motivation
What are your initial reasons for wanting to create a post? Why do you want to be on Social Media in the first place?

- To introduce yourself and/or your business; i.e. move people from not knowing you exist to knowing you exist
- To let people get to know more about you and your business
- To be seen as a go-to source for your topic or industry
- To build an ongoing connection
- To generate specific interest? What kind of specific interest?
- To educate
- To inspire
- To raise awareness about a certain cause or topic
- Increase overall visibility and reach
- Connect with a new segment of your potential customers/clients
- Provide added value for existing clients/customers
- Build a community
- Build and solidify your reputation
- Other

## Your Followers
Who is your ideal follower?
The biggest hurdle for developing Social Media content is to understand what your ideal follower wants from you in this space. The better you know your ideal follower, the more chance you have to give them something they actually want (as opposed to what you think they should want or what you want them to want). The goal here is to understand, as much as possible, who your followers are and what is important to them. Digging deep will give you ideas about how you might use Social Media to add real value to their lives.

Keep in mind the real power of Social Media lies is engagement. It is your special opportunity to serve your followers and make a connection with them. You want your Social Media posts to relate to your followers' own wants and needs. Creating content that is valuable to your followers is how you will earn their attention and motivate them to move closer to you, visit your site, follow your Instagram, check out your Facebook page, etc. Think of it as nurturing your garden by giving the plants what they need in order to flourish. Here are a few questions to help you learn more about your ideal followers:

Who do you help?

What types of things are they interested in?

What do they want most?

What is holding them back?

What kinds of mistakes do they make?

What do they not know that they should know?

What have they tried & failed?

What are they afraid of?

What does "remaining stuck" cost them now and in the future?

Where do they hang out online? Here are a couple of helpful links:
http://www.pewinternet.org/2018/03/01/social-media-use-in-2018/
http://www.pewinternet.org/2018/03/01/social-media-use-in-2018/pi_2018-03-01_social-media_a-01/

What social networks do theyprimarily use?

What entertains them?

Where and how do they currently get information related to your niche?

Who or what influences them? What are they fans of?

What kinds of questions are they asking in your niche? You can use sites like Quora.com
https://www.quora.com/ or Yahoo Answers https://answers.yahoo.com/ to help you find out.

# General Demographics

Where do they live? Are they local to you? In the neighborhood or neighboring town? State? Country? Or not at all geographically defined?

Gender?

Age or age range?

Income?

Family size?

What family role? Parent? Child? Grandparent? Etc.

Education?

Occupation(s)?

Work? Retired, employed? Unemployed? Underemployed?

Other?

# All About You

Who are You? What is your own story?

What is your USP (unique selling proposition)? What makes you different than others in your field?

What are some ways you might communicate who you are and what you stand for via Social Media without lecturing or selling?

Do you already have an online presence? If so, who is talking about you and what are they saying? Try using:
Twitter Advanced Search https://twitter.com/search-advanced
Google Alerts https://www.google.com/alerts
SocialMention http://www.socialmention.com/
BoardReader http://boardreader.com

What did you learn? Do these people fit or overlap your ideal follower profile?

# Brainstorming Post Content Ideas

Using paper, a spreadsheet, note-taking app or whatever you wish, make a list of ANY kind of content that you have ever created.

## What do you already know?

Set a timer to 3 minutes. Quickly write down a list of what you already know, are currently learning, or are working on. How can you use what you're already doing as a way to help people and add value to their lives.

## What do you want to know?

Set a timer to 3 minutes. Quickly write down a list of any course you plan to take or would like to take, non fiction books you have been planning to read, topics you've been wanting to educate yourself about.

## Extemporaneous Brainstorming

Using mind-mapping, Free-writing, voice recorder while taking a walk, doodling or ???, to brainstorm Blog and Social Media post ideas. Reserve any judgment until after your brainstorming session is over.

## Review your lists

Review your lists. Circle anything that jumps out at you. Make a "Short List." Sleep on it. When you wake up, ask yourself which ideas would be the most fun? The most helpful? The most evergreen? If you want to, make a vin diagram. Put the things that your ideal follower would be most likely to be interested in on one side and your top ideas for your Blog & Social Media posts on the other side. Where do they overlap?

## Identify Your Business Goals

What specific outcomes are you looking for? What are some actions you want your ideal follower to eventually take in response to your posts? Here are some ideas:

Visit your website

Like your Facebook page

Join a Facebook Group

Follow you on Twitter

Follow you on Instagram

Connect with you on some other social media platform Which one?

Subscribe to your Podcast

Sign up to your Email List

Call you

Fill out a contact form

Schedule an appointment

Register for an Event

Request Information

Ask for a Quote

Visit Your Business Location

Take a Survey

Make a Donation

Other Actions:

# Handy Reference

## Social Media Image Sizes

### Instagram

| Instagram | Recommended Dimensions: | Aspect Ratio |
|---|---|---|
| Profile Picture | 110 x 110 | - |
| Photo Thumbnails | 161 x 161 | - |
| Photo Size (Instagram App) | 1080 x 1080 (square), 1080 x 1350 (4:5) | Between 1.91:1 and 4:5 |
| Instagram Stories | 1080 x 1920 | 9:16 |
| | | |

### Facebook

| Facebook | Recommended Dimensions: | Minimum Dimensions: | Maximum Dimensions: | Image Scale: | Max File Size: | Image Formats: |
|---|---|---|---|---|---|---|
| Profile Photo | 180 x 180 | 160 x 160 | - | 1:1 | - | - |
| Cover Photo | T 820 x 312 | 400 x 150 | - | 2.7:1 | 100KB | RGB, JPG, PNG |
| Shared Image (Timeline) | 1200 x 630 | - | - | 1.91:1 | - | - |
| Shared Image (Newsfeed) | 1200 x 630 | - | - | 1.91:1 | - | - |
| Shared Link (Timeline) | 1200 x 628 | 200 x 200 | - | 1.91:1 | - | - |
| Shared Link (Newsfeed) | 1200 x 628 | 200 x 200 | - | 1.91:1 | - | - |
| Highlighted Image | 1200 x 717 | 843 x 504 | - | 1:1.67 | - | - |
| Event Image | 1920 x 1080 | 470 x 174 | - | 16:9 | - | - |

## Twitter

| Twitter | Recommended Dimensions: | Minimum Dimensions: | Maximum Dimensions: | Image Scale: | Max File Size: | Image Formats: |
|---|---|---|---|---|---|---|
| Profile Photo: | 400 x 400 | 200 x 200 | - | 1:1 | 2MB | JPG, GIF, PNG |
| Header Photo: | 1500 x 500 | - | - | 3:1 | 5MB | JPG, GIF, PNG |
| In-Stream Photo: | 506 x 253 | 440 x 220 | 1024 x 512 | 2:1 | 5MB for Photos, 3 MB for Gifs | JPG, GIF, PNG |

## Pinterest

| Pinterest | Recommended Dimensions: | Appears at (height scaled): | Maximum File Size: | Image Formats: |
|---|---|---|---|---|
| Profile Picture | 165 x 165 | 165 x 165 | 10MB | JPG, PNG |
| Pins (main page) | 236 | 192 | - | - |
| Pins (on board) | 236 | 238 | - | - |
| Pins (expanded) | 600 Width | 735 | - | - |
| Pins (enlarged pin) | - | 500 (infinite height) | - | - |
| Pin Board (large thumbnail) | 222 x 150 | - | - | - |
| Pin Board (smaller thumbnail) | 55 x 55 | - | - | - |

## Tumblr

| Tumblr | Recommended Dimensions: | File Format | Maximum Size |
|---|---|---|---|
| Profile Picture | 128 x 128 | JPG, GIF, PNG, BMP | 10MB |
| Image Posts (In Dash) | 1280 x 1920 | JPG, GIF, PNG, BMP | 10MB |
| Image Posts (In Feed) | 500 x 750 | JPG, GIF, PNG, BMP | 10MB |
| Animated Gifs | Maximum 540px Wide | JPG, GIF, PNG, BMP | 3MB |

# Youtube

| Youtube | Recommended Dimensions: | Aspect Ratio |
|---|---|---|
| Channel Profile Image | 800 x 800 | - |
| Channel Cover Art | 2560 x 1440 | - |
| Tablet | 1855 x 423 | - |
| Mobile | 1546 x 423 | - |
| TV | 2560 x 1440 | - |
| Desktop | 2560 x 423 | - |
| Video Uploads | Minimum HD 1280 x 720 | 16:9 |

# LinkedIn

| LinkedIn | Recommended Dimensions: | Appears at (height scaled): | Maximum File Size | File Format |
|---|---|---|---|---|
| Personal Profile Image | 400 x 400 | 500 x 500 | 8MB | PNG, JPG, GIF |
| Personal Background Image | 1584 x 396 | 1400 x 425 | 4MB | PNG, JPG, GIF |
| Company Logo Image | 300 x 300 | 110 x 110 | 4MB | PNG, JPG, GIF |
| Square Logo | 60 x 60 | 60 x 60 | 2MB | PNG, JPG, GIF |
| Company Cover Image | 1536 x 768 | 1400 x 425 | 4MB | PNG, JPG, GIF |
| Banner Image | 646 x 220 | 646 x 220 | 2MB | PNG, JPG, GIF |
| Hero Photo | 1536 x 768 | varies between desktop and mobile | 2MB | PNG, JPG, GIF |
| Shared Link | 1104 x 736 | 552 x 289 | - | PNG, JPG, GIF |
| Shared Image | 1104 x 736 | varies between desktop and mobile | - | PNG, JPG, GIF |
| Company Photos | 900 x 600 | 900 x 600 | - | PNG, JPG, GIF |

# Days of the Week Hashtags

Days of the Week hashtags are a great way to get in front of new people and get new followers. Here are some examples:

## Monday Hashtags
#Mondaymantra #Mondaymotivation #Mondaymood #Mondayblues #Mondayfunday #Shootfilmonmondays #meatfreemonday #Mondaymemories #Mondaymadness #Mindfulmonday #Manicmonday #Marketingmonday #Mancrushmonday (#mcm) #Musicmonday

## Tuesday Hashtags
#Tuesdaythoughts #Transformationtuesday #Tuesdaytip #Tuesdaytruth #Tuesdaytreat #Tuesdaytrivia #Turtletuesday #Tuesdaytunes #Tuesdaytakeover #Tongueouttuesday #Tattootuesday #Traveltuesday #Goodnewstuesday #Tastingtuesday

## Wednesday Hashtags
#Wednesdaywisdom #Wednesdayworkout #Wednesdaywords #Wednesdaywellness #Winitwednesday #Waterfallwednesday #Whiskerswednesday #Weddingwednesday #Womancrushwednesday (#wcw) #Waybackwednesday

## Thursday Hashtags
#Thursdaythoughts #Thursdaythrowpillows #Handtoolthursday #Throwbackthursday (#TBT) #Tacothursday #Thoughtfulthursday #Thursdaytreat #Thirstythursday #Thankfulthursday #Thursdate #Thursdayvibes #Thursdayquotes #Thursdayparty #Thursdaymorning #Thursdaynight

## Friday Hashtags
#Fridayfeeling #Fridayvibes #Fridayintroductions #Fridaysforfuture #Fridayfeels #Fridayfunny #Fridayflowers #Fanartfriday #Fridayfitness #Blackfriday #Fitfriday #TGIF #Fearlessfriday #Foodiefriday #Fridayfacts

## Saturday Hashtags
#Saturdaybrunch #Saturdaystyle #Saturdayshenanigans #Saturdayselfie #Saturdaynightfever #Caturday #Saturdaysale #Saturdayshoutout #Saturdayswag #Saturdayrun #Saturdayfun #Saturdaymotivation #Saturdayparty #Selfcaresaturday #Saturdayshopping #Screenshotsaturday

## Sunday Hashtags
#Spotlightsunday #Sciencesunday #Sundayvibes #Sundayscaries #Sundayfunday #Sundaybaking #Pancakesunday #Supersoulsunday #Startupsunday #Sundaysweat #Sundayreads #Sundaybest #Sundaydinner #Sundaysesh #Sundayhike #Sundayroast

# Best Times to Post

The best times to post depend on your ideal follower, when they are online, whenever it is most relevant to them. This can change. For more detailed information, check out this study: https://sproutsocial.com/insights/best-times-to-post-on-social-media/

Meanwhile, the following can act as a starting point:

| Platform | Day | Times |
|----------|-----|-------|
| Facebook | Wednesday | Noon and 2 p.m. |
|  | Thursday | 1 and 2 p.m. |
| Instagram | Wednesday | 3 p.m. |
|  | Thursday | 5 a.m., 11 a.m. and 3–4 p.m. |
|  | Friday | 5 a.m. |
| LinkedIn | Wednesday | 3–5 p.m. |
| Pinterest | Friday and Saturday | 8–11 p.m., 2–4 a.m. and 2–4 p.m. |
| Twitter | Friday | 9–10 a.m. |

# Social Media / Hashtag Holidays

Social Media Hashtag Holidays are a great way to inspire and add fun to your content. Googling "hashtag holidays" will return some great resources. Also, here are some sites for browsing fun, non-traditional events, holidays and observances

- checkiday.com
- daysoftheyear.com
- eventguide.com
- holidayinsights.com
- holidays-and-observances.com
- holidayscalendar.com
- nationaldaycalendar.com
- nationaltoday.com
- whatnationaldayisit.com

Following is a handy at-a-glance calendar where you can keep track of and add selected holidays and observances. (Be sure to add important dates and events relevant to YOUR industry.)

## Special Dates, Holidays, Observances

### January

1 #NewYearsDay
21 #NationalHugDay

### February

2 #GroundhogDay
14 #ValentinesDay

### March

14 #PiDay
17 #StPatricksDay

### July

4 #4thOfJuly
17 #WorldEmojiDay

### August

8 #CatDay
26 #NationalDogDay

### September

11 #NeverForget
#September11th

## April

1 #AprilFoolsDay
#AprilFools
15 #TaxDay

## May

4 #StarWarsDay
#MayThe4thBeWithYou
5 #CincoDeMayo

## June

21 #NationalSelfieDay
23 #NationalPinkDay

## October

31 #Halloween
#HappyHalloween

## November

11 #VeteransDay
19 #MensDay

## December

24 #ChristmasEve
25 #MerryChristmas
31 #NYE #NewYearsEve

## Post Ideas Worksheet

Post Pub Date _____ Platform _____

Topic _____ Type _____

Hashtags/Keywords _____

Notes _____

_____

_____

_____

Post Pub Date _____ Platform _____

Topic _____ Type _____

Hashtags/Keywords _____

Notes _____

_____

_____

_____

Post Pub Date _____ Platform _____

Topic _____ Type _____

Hashtags/Keywords _____

Notes _____

_____

_____

_____

Post Pub Date _____ Platform _____

Topic _____ Type _____

Hashtags/Keywords _____

Notes _____

_____

_____

_____

Post Pub Date _____ Platform _____

Topic _____ Type _____

Hashtags/Keywords _____

Notes _____

_____

_____

_____

---

Post Pub Date _____ Platform _____

Topic _____ Type _____

Hashtags/Keywords _____

Notes _____

_____

_____

_____

---

Post Pub Date _____ Platform _____

Topic _____ Type _____

Hashtags/Keywords _____

Notes _____

_____

_____

_____

---

Post Pub Date _____ Platform _____

Topic _____ Type _____

Hashtags/Keywords _____

Notes _____

_____

_____

_____

## Social Media Schedule

Week of _____

This Week's Focus _____

_____

| | Monday | Tuesday | Wednesday |
|---|---|---|---|
| Theme | | | |
| Platform & Post Time | | | |
| | | | |
| | | | |
| | | | |
| | | | |

Hashtags/Keywords

| Thursday | Friday | Saturday | Sunday |
|---|---|---|---|
|  |  |  |  |
|  |  |  |  |
|  |  |  |  |
|  |  |  |  |
|  |  |  |  |
|  |  |  |  |

▶ Post Ideas Worksheet

Post Pub Date _____ Platform _____
Topic _____ Type _____
Hashtags/Keywords _____
Notes _____
_____
_____
_____

Post Pub Date _____ Platform _____
Topic _____ Type _____
Hashtags/Keywords _____
Notes _____
_____
_____
_____

Post Pub Date _____ Platform _____
Topic _____ Type _____
Hashtags/Keywords _____
Notes _____
_____
_____
_____

Post Pub Date _____ Platform _____
Topic _____ Type _____
Hashtags/Keywords _____
Notes _____
_____
_____
_____

Post Pub Date _____ Platform _____

Topic _____ Type _____

Hashtags/Keywords _____

Notes _____

_____

_____

Post Pub Date _____ Platform _____

Topic _____ Type _____

Hashtags/Keywords _____

Notes _____

_____

_____

Post Pub Date _____ Platform _____

Topic _____ Type _____

Hashtags/Keywords _____

Notes _____

_____

_____

Post Pub Date _____ Platform _____

Topic _____ Type _____

Hashtags/Keywords _____

Notes _____

_____

_____

# Social Media Schedule

Week of _____

This Week's Focus _____

_____

| | Monday | Tuesday | Wednesday |
|---|---|---|---|
| **Theme** | | | |
| **Platform & Post Time** | | | |
| | | | |
| | | | |
| | | | |
| | | | |
| | | | |

Hashtags/Keywords

| Thursday | Friday | Saturday | Sunday |
|----------|--------|----------|--------|
|          |        |          |        |
|          |        |          |        |
|          |        |          |        |
|          |        |          |        |
|          |        |          |        |
|          |        |          |        |

## Post Ideas Worksheet

Post Pub Date _____ Platform _____

Topic _____ Type _____

Hashtags/Keywords _____

Notes _____

_____

_____

_____


Post Pub Date _____ Platform _____

Topic _____ Type _____

Hashtags/Keywords _____

Notes _____

_____

_____

_____


Post Pub Date _____ Platform _____

Topic _____ Type _____

Hashtags/Keywords _____

Notes _____

_____

_____

_____


Post Pub Date _____ Platform _____

Topic _____ Type _____

Hashtags/Keywords _____

Notes _____

_____

_____

_____

Post Pub Date _____ Platform _____

Topic _____ Type _____

Hashtags/Keywords _____

Notes _____

_____

_____

---

Post Pub Date _____ Platform _____

Topic _____ Type _____

Hashtags/Keywords _____

Notes _____

_____

_____

---

Post Pub Date _____ Platform _____

Topic _____ Type _____

Hashtags/Keywords _____

Notes _____

_____

_____

---

Post Pub Date _____ Platform _____

Topic _____ Type _____

Hashtags/Keywords _____

Notes _____

_____

_____

# Social Media Schedule

Week of _____

This Week's Focus _____

_____

| | Monday | Tuesday | Wednesday |
|---|---|---|---|
| **Theme** | | | |
| **Platform & Post Time** | | | |
| | | | |
| | | | |
| | | | |
| | | | |

Hashtags/Keywords _____

_____

_____

| Thursday | Friday | Saturday | Sunday |
|---|---|---|---|
| | | | |
| | | | |
| | | | |
| | | | |
| | | | |
| | | | |

Post Pub Date _____  Platform _____

Topic _____  Type _____

Hashtags/Keywords _____

Notes _____

_____

_____

_____

Post Pub Date _____  Platform _____

Topic _____  Type _____

Hashtags/Keywords _____

Notes _____

_____

_____

_____

Post Pub Date _____  Platform _____

Topic _____  Type _____

Hashtags/Keywords _____

Notes _____

_____

_____

_____

Post Pub Date _____  Platform _____

Topic _____  Type _____

Hashtags/Keywords _____

Notes _____

_____

_____

_____

Post Pub Date _____ Platform _____

Topic _____ Type _____

Hashtags/Keywords _____

Notes _____

_____

_____

_____

---

Post Pub Date _____ Platform _____

Topic _____ Type _____

Hashtags/Keywords _____

Notes _____

_____

_____

_____

---

Post Pub Date _____ Platform _____

Topic _____ Type _____

Hashtags/Keywords _____

Notes _____

_____

_____

_____

---

Post Pub Date _____ Platform _____

Topic _____ Type _____

Hashtags/Keywords _____

Notes _____

_____

_____

_____

# Social Media Schedule

Week of _____

This Week's Focus _____

_____

| | Monday | Tuesday | Wednesday |
|---|---|---|---|
| Theme | | | |
| Platform & Post Time | | | |
| | | | |
| | | | |
| | | | |
| | | | |

| Thursday | Friday | Saturday | Sunday |
|----------|--------|----------|--------|
|          |        |          |        |
|          |        |          |        |
|          |        |          |        |
|          |        |          |        |
|          |        |          |        |
|          |        |          |        |

## Post Ideas Worksheet

Post Pub Date _____ Platform _____

Topic _____ Type _____

Hashtags/Keywords _____

Notes _____
_____
_____

Post Pub Date _____ Platform _____

Topic _____ Type _____

Hashtags/Keywords _____

Notes _____
_____
_____

Post Pub Date _____ Platform _____

Topic _____ Type _____

Hashtags/Keywords _____

Notes _____
_____
_____

Post Pub Date _____ Platform _____

Topic _____ Type _____

Hashtags/Keywords _____

Notes _____
_____
_____

Post Pub Date _____ Platform _____

Topic _____ Type _____

Hashtags/Keywords _____

Notes _____

_____

_____

Post Pub Date _____ Platform _____

Topic _____ Type _____

Hashtags/Keywords _____

Notes _____

_____

_____

Post Pub Date _____ Platform _____

Topic _____ Type _____

Hashtags/Keywords _____

Notes _____

_____

_____

Post Pub Date _____ Platform _____

Topic _____ Type _____

Hashtags/Keywords _____

Notes _____

_____

_____

# Social Media Schedule

Week of _____

This Week's Focus _____

_____

|  | Monday | Tuesday | Wednesday |
|---|---|---|---|
| Theme |  |  |  |
| Platform & Post Time |  |  |  |
|  |  |  |  |
|  |  |  |  |
|  |  |  |  |
|  |  |  |  |

| Thursday | Friday | Saturday | Sunday |
|---|---|---|---|
| | | | |
| | | | |
| | | | |
| | | | |
| | | | |
| | | | |

## Post Ideas Worksheet

Post Pub Date _____ Platform _____

Topic _____ Type _____

Hashtags/Keywords _____

Notes _____

_____

_____

Post Pub Date _____ Platform _____

Topic _____ Type _____

Hashtags/Keywords _____

Notes _____

_____

_____

Post Pub Date _____ Platform _____

Topic _____ Type _____

Hashtags/Keywords _____

Notes _____

_____

_____

Post Pub Date _____ Platform _____

Topic _____ Type _____

Hashtags/Keywords _____

Notes _____

_____

_____

Post Pub Date _____ Platform _____

Topic _____ Type _____

Hashtags/Keywords _____

Notes _____

_____

_____

_____

Post Pub Date _____ Platform _____

Topic _____ Type _____

Hashtags/Keywords _____

Notes _____

_____

_____

_____

Post Pub Date _____ Platform _____

Topic _____ Type _____

Hashtags/Keywords _____

Notes _____

_____

_____

_____

Post Pub Date _____ Platform _____

Topic _____ Type _____

Hashtags/Keywords _____

Notes _____

_____

_____

_____

## Social Media Schedule

Week of _____

This Week's Focus _____

_____

| | Monday | Tuesday | Wednesday |
|---|---|---|---|
| Theme | | | |
| Platform & Post Time | | | |
| | | | |
| | | | |
| | | | |
| | | | |

## Hashtags/Keywords

| Thursday | Friday | Saturday | Sunday |
|----------|--------|----------|--------|
|          |        |          |        |
|          |        |          |        |
|          |        |          |        |
|          |        |          |        |
|          |        |          |        |
|          |        |          |        |

## Post Ideas Worksheet

Post Pub Date _____  Platform _____

Topic _____  Type _____

Hashtags/Keywords _____

Notes _____

_____

_____

Post Pub Date _____  Platform _____

Topic _____  Type _____

Hashtags/Keywords _____

Notes _____

_____

_____

Post Pub Date _____  Platform _____

Topic _____  Type _____

Hashtags/Keywords _____

Notes _____

_____

_____

Post Pub Date _____  Platform _____

Topic _____  Type _____

Hashtags/Keywords _____

Notes _____

_____

_____

Post Pub Date _____ Platform _____

Topic _____ Type _____

Hashtags/Keywords _____

Notes _____

_____

_____

_____

Post Pub Date _____ Platform _____

Topic _____ Type _____

Hashtags/Keywords _____

Notes _____

_____

_____

_____

Post Pub Date _____ Platform _____

Topic _____ Type _____

Hashtags/Keywords _____

Notes _____

_____

_____

_____

Post Pub Date _____ Platform _____

Topic _____ Type _____

Hashtags/Keywords _____

Notes _____

_____

_____

_____

## Social Media Schedule

Week of _____

This Week's Focus _____

_____

|  | Monday | Tuesday | Wednesday |
|---|---|---|---|
| Theme | | | |
| Platform & Post Time | | | |
| | | | |
| | | | |
| | | | |
| | | | |
| | | | |

Hashtags/Keywords

| Thursday | Friday | Saturday | Sunday |
|----------|--------|----------|--------|
|          |        |          |        |
|          |        |          |        |
|          |        |          |        |
|          |        |          |        |
|          |        |          |        |
|          |        |          |        |

## Post Ideas Worksheet

Post Pub Date _____  Platform _____

Topic _____  Type _____

Hashtags/Keywords _____

Notes _____

_____

_____

Post Pub Date _____  Platform _____

Topic _____  Type _____

Hashtags/Keywords _____

Notes _____

_____

_____

Post Pub Date _____  Platform _____

Topic _____  Type _____

Hashtags/Keywords _____

Notes _____

_____

_____

Post Pub Date _____  Platform _____

Topic _____  Type _____

Hashtags/Keywords _____

Notes _____

_____

_____

Post Pub Date _____ Platform _____

Topic _____ Type _____

Hashtags/Keywords _____

Notes _____

_____

_____

_____

Post Pub Date _____ Platform _____

Topic _____ Type _____

Hashtags/Keywords _____

Notes _____

_____

_____

_____

Post Pub Date _____ Platform _____

Topic _____ Type _____

Hashtags/Keywords _____

Notes _____

_____

_____

_____

Post Pub Date _____ Platform _____

Topic _____ Type _____

Hashtags/Keywords _____

Notes _____

_____

_____

_____

# Social Media Schedule

Week of _____

This Week's Focus _____

_____

| | Monday | Tuesday | Wednesday |
|---|---|---|---|
| Theme | | | |
| Platform & Post Time | | | |
| | | | |
| | | | |
| | | | |
| | | | |
| | | | |

## Hashtags/Keywords

| Thursday | Friday | Saturday | Sunday |
|----------|--------|----------|--------|
|          |        |          |        |
|          |        |          |        |
|          |        |          |        |
|          |        |          |        |
|          |        |          |        |
|          |        |          |        |

## Post Ideas Worksheet

Post Pub Date _____    Platform _____

Topic _____    Type _____

Hashtags/Keywords _____

Notes _____

_____

_____

---

Post Pub Date _____    Platform _____

Topic _____    Type _____

Hashtags/Keywords _____

Notes _____

_____

_____

---

Post Pub Date _____    Platform _____

Topic _____    Type _____

Hashtags/Keywords _____

Notes _____

_____

_____

---

Post Pub Date _____    Platform _____

Topic _____    Type _____

Hashtags/Keywords _____

Notes _____

_____

_____

**Post Pub Date** _____  **Platform** _____

**Topic** _____  **Type** _____

**Hashtags/Keywords** _____

**Notes** _____

_____

_____

_____

---

**Post Pub Date** _____  **Platform** _____

**Topic** _____  **Type** _____

**Hashtags/Keywords** _____

**Notes** _____

_____

_____

_____

---

**Post Pub Date** _____  **Platform** _____

**Topic** _____  **Type** _____

**Hashtags/Keywords** _____

**Notes** _____

_____

_____

_____

---

**Post Pub Date** _____  **Platform** _____

**Topic** _____  **Type** _____

**Hashtags/Keywords** _____

**Notes** _____

_____

_____

_____

# Social Media Schedule

Week of _____

This Week's Focus _____

_____

| | Monday | Tuesday | Wednesday |
|---|---|---|---|
| Theme | | | |
| Platform & Post Time | | | |
| | | | |
| | | | |
| | | | |
| | | | |
| | | | |

| Thursday | Friday | Saturday | Sunday |
|----------|--------|----------|--------|
|          |        |          |        |
|          |        |          |        |
|          |        |          |        |
|          |        |          |        |
|          |        |          |        |
|          |        |          |        |

## Post Ideas Worksheet

Post Pub Date _____ Platform _____

Topic _____ Type _____

Hashtags/Keywords _____

Notes _____

_____

_____

Post Pub Date _____ Platform _____

Topic _____ Type _____

Hashtags/Keywords _____

Notes _____

_____

_____

Post Pub Date _____ Platform _____

Topic _____ Type _____

Hashtags/Keywords _____

Notes _____

_____

_____

Post Pub Date _____ Platform _____

Topic _____ Type _____

Hashtags/Keywords _____

Notes _____

_____

_____

Post Pub Date _____  Platform _____

Topic _____  Type _____

Hashtags/Keywords _____

Notes _____

_____

_____

Post Pub Date _____  Platform _____

Topic _____  Type _____

Hashtags/Keywords _____

Notes _____

_____

_____

Post Pub Date _____  Platform _____

Topic _____  Type _____

Hashtags/Keywords _____

Notes _____

_____

_____

Post Pub Date _____  Platform _____

Topic _____  Type _____

Hashtags/Keywords _____

Notes _____

_____

_____

Week of _____

This Week's Focus _____

_____

| | Monday | Tuesday | Wednesday |
|---|---|---|---|
| Theme | | | |
| Platform & Post Time | | | |
| | | | |
| | | | |
| | | | |
| | | | |
| | | | |

Hashtags/Keywords_____

_____

_____

| Thursday | Friday | Saturday | Sunday |
|----------|--------|----------|--------|
|          |        |          |        |
|          |        |          |        |
|          |        |          |        |
|          |        |          |        |
|          |        |          |        |
|          |        |          |        |

Post Pub Date _____ Platform _____

Topic _____ Type _____

Hashtags/Keywords _____

Notes _____

_____

_____

_____

Post Pub Date _____ Platform _____

Topic _____ Type _____

Hashtags/Keywords _____

Notes _____

_____

_____

_____

Post Pub Date _____ Platform _____

Topic _____ Type _____

Hashtags/Keywords _____

Notes _____

_____

_____

_____

Post Pub Date _____ Platform _____

Topic _____ Type _____

Hashtags/Keywords _____

Notes _____

_____

_____

_____

Post Pub Date _____ Platform _____

Topic _____ Type _____

Hashtags/Keywords _____

Notes _____

_____

_____

_____

Post Pub Date _____ Platform _____

Topic _____ Type _____

Hashtags/Keywords _____

Notes _____

_____

_____

_____

Post Pub Date _____ Platform _____

Topic _____ Type _____

Hashtags/Keywords _____

Notes _____

_____

_____

_____

Post Pub Date _____ Platform _____

Topic _____ Type _____

Hashtags/Keywords _____

Notes _____

_____

_____

_____

# Social Media Schedule

Week of _____

This Week's Focus _____

_____

|  | Monday | Tuesday | Wednesday |
|---|---|---|---|
| Theme | | | |
| Platform & Post Time | | | |
| | | | |
| | | | |
| | | | |
| | | | |
| | | | |

| Thursday | Friday | Saturday | Sunday |
|----------|--------|----------|--------|
|          |        |          |        |
|          |        |          |        |
|          |        |          |        |
|          |        |          |        |
|          |        |          |        |
|          |        |          |        |

## ▶ Post Ideas Worksheet

Post Pub Date _____ Platform _____

Topic _____ Type _____

Hashtags/Keywords _____

Notes _____

_____

_____

---

Post Pub Date _____ Platform _____

Topic _____ Type _____

Hashtags/Keywords _____

Notes _____

_____

_____

---

Post Pub Date _____ Platform _____

Topic _____ Type _____

Hashtags/Keywords _____

Notes _____

_____

_____

---

Post Pub Date _____ Platform _____

Topic _____ Type _____

Hashtags/Keywords _____

Notes _____

_____

_____

Post Pub Date _____ Platform _____

Topic _____ Type _____

Hashtags/Keywords _____

Notes _____

_____

_____

_____


Post Pub Date _____ Platform _____

Topic _____ Type _____

Hashtags/Keywords _____

Notes _____

_____

_____

_____


Post Pub Date _____ Platform _____

Topic _____ Type _____

Hashtags/Keywords _____

Notes _____

_____

_____

_____


Post Pub Date _____ Platform _____

Topic _____ Type _____

Hashtags/Keywords _____

Notes _____

_____

_____

_____

# Social Media Schedule

Week of _____

This Week's Focus _____
_____

| | Monday | Tuesday | Wednesday |
|---|---|---|---|
| Theme | | | |
| Platform & Post Time | | | |
| | | | |
| | | | |
| | | | |
| | | | |
| | | | |

| Thursday | Friday | Saturday | Sunday |
|----------|--------|----------|--------|
|          |        |          |        |
|          |        |          |        |
|          |        |          |        |
|          |        |          |        |
|          |        |          |        |
|          |        |          |        |

Post Pub Date _____ Platform _____

Topic _____ Type _____

Hashtags/Keywords _____

Notes _____

_____

_____

---

Post Pub Date _____ Platform _____

Topic _____ Type _____

Hashtags/Keywords _____

Notes _____

_____

_____

---

Post Pub Date _____ Platform _____

Topic _____ Type _____

Hashtags/Keywords _____

Notes _____

_____

_____

---

Post Pub Date _____ Platform _____

Topic _____ Type _____

Hashtags/Keywords _____

Notes _____

_____

_____

Post Pub Date _____ Platform _____

Topic _____ Type _____

Hashtags/Keywords _____

Notes _____

_____

_____

_____

Post Pub Date _____ Platform _____

Topic _____ Type _____

Hashtags/Keywords _____

Notes _____

_____

_____

_____

Post Pub Date _____ Platform _____

Topic _____ Type _____

Hashtags/Keywords _____

Notes _____

_____

_____

_____

Post Pub Date _____ Platform _____

Topic _____ Type _____

Hashtags/Keywords _____

Notes _____

_____

_____

_____

> Social Media Schedule

Week of _____

This Week's Focus _____
_____
_____

| | Monday | Tuesday | Wednesday |
|---|---|---|---|
| Theme | | | |
| Platform & Post Time | | | |
| | | | |
| | | | |
| | | | |
| | | | |
| | | | |

| Thursday | Friday | Saturday | Sunday |
|----------|--------|----------|--------|
|  |  |  |  |
|  |  |  |  |
|  |  |  |  |
|  |  |  |  |
|  |  |  |  |
|  |  |  |  |

Post Pub Date _____ Platform _____

Topic _____ Type _____

Hashtags/Keywords _____

Notes _____

_____

_____

_____

Post Pub Date _____ Platform _____

Topic _____ Type _____

Hashtags/Keywords _____

Notes _____

_____

_____

_____

Post Pub Date _____ Platform _____

Topic _____ Type _____

Hashtags/Keywords _____

Notes _____

_____

_____

_____

Post Pub Date _____ Platform _____

Topic _____ Type _____

Hashtags/Keywords _____

Notes _____

_____

_____

_____

Post Pub Date _____ Platform _____

Topic _____ Type _____

Hashtags/Keywords _____

Notes _____

_____

_____

_____

Post Pub Date _____ Platform _____

Topic _____ Type _____

Hashtags/Keywords _____

Notes _____

_____

_____

_____

Post Pub Date _____ Platform _____

Topic _____ Type _____

Hashtags/Keywords _____

Notes _____

_____

_____

_____

Post Pub Date _____ Platform _____

Topic _____ Type _____

Hashtags/Keywords _____

Notes _____

_____

_____

_____

# Social Media Schedule

Week of _____

This Week's Focus _____

_____

| | Monday | Tuesday | Wednesday |
|---|---|---|---|
| Theme | | | |
| Platform & Post Time | | | |
| | | | |
| | | | |
| | | | |
| | | | |
| | | | |

| Thursday | Friday | Saturday | Sunday |
|---|---|---|---|
| | | | |
| | | | |
| | | | |
| | | | |
| | | | |
| | | | |

## Post Ideas Worksheet

Post Pub Date _____ Platform _____

Topic _____ Type _____

Hashtags/Keywords _____

Notes _____

_____

_____

_____

---

Post Pub Date _____ Platform _____

Topic _____ Type _____

Hashtags/Keywords _____

Notes _____

_____

_____

_____

---

Post Pub Date _____ Platform _____

Topic _____ Type _____

Hashtags/Keywords _____

Notes _____

_____

_____

_____

---

Post Pub Date _____ Platform _____

Topic _____ Type _____

Hashtags/Keywords _____

Notes _____

_____

_____

_____

Post Pub Date _____ Platform _____

Topic _____ Type _____

Hashtags/Keywords _____

Notes _____

_____

_____

Post Pub Date _____ Platform _____

Topic _____ Type _____

Hashtags/Keywords _____

Notes _____

_____

_____

Post Pub Date _____ Platform _____

Topic _____ Type _____

Hashtags/Keywords _____

Notes _____

_____

_____

Post Pub Date _____ Platform _____

Topic _____ Type _____

Hashtags/Keywords _____

Notes _____

_____

_____

# Social Media Schedule

Week of _____

This Week's Focus _____

_____

| | Monday | Tuesday | Wednesday |
|---|---|---|---|
| Theme | | | |
| Platform & Post Time | | | |
| | | | |
| | | | |
| | | | |
| | | | |
| | | | |

| Thursday | Friday | Saturday | Sunday |
|---|---|---|---|
|  |  |  |  |
|  |  |  |  |
|  |  |  |  |
|  |  |  |  |
|  |  |  |  |
|  |  |  |  |

## Post Ideas Worksheet

Post Pub Date _____ Platform _____

Topic _____ Type _____

Hashtags/Keywords _____

Notes _____

_____

_____

_____

Post Pub Date _____ Platform _____

Topic _____ Type _____

Hashtags/Keywords _____

Notes _____

_____

_____

_____

Post Pub Date _____ Platform _____

Topic _____ Type _____

Hashtags/Keywords _____

Notes _____

_____

_____

_____

Post Pub Date _____ Platform _____

Topic _____ Type _____

Hashtags/Keywords _____

Notes _____

_____

_____

_____

Post Pub Date _____ Platform _____

Topic _____ Type _____

Hashtags/Keywords _____

Notes _____

_____

_____

_____

Post Pub Date _____ Platform _____

Topic _____ Type _____

Hashtags/Keywords _____

Notes _____

_____

_____

_____

Post Pub Date _____ Platform _____

Topic _____ Type _____

Hashtags/Keywords _____

Notes _____

_____

_____

_____

Post Pub Date _____ Platform _____

Topic _____ Type _____

Hashtags/Keywords _____

Notes _____

_____

_____

_____

# Social Media Schedule

Week of _____

This Week's Focus _____

_____

|  | Monday | Tuesday | Wednesday |
|---|---|---|---|
| Theme |  |  |  |
| Platform & Post Time |  |  |  |
|  |  |  |  |
|  |  |  |  |
|  |  |  |  |
|  |  |  |  |
|  |  |  |  |

## Hashtags/Keywords

| Thursday | Friday | Saturday | Sunday |
|----------|--------|----------|--------|
|          |        |          |        |
|          |        |          |        |
|          |        |          |        |
|          |        |          |        |
|          |        |          |        |
|          |        |          |        |

## Post Ideas Worksheet

Post Pub Date _____ Platform _____

Topic _____ Type _____

Hashtags/Keywords _____

Notes _____

_____

_____

_____

Post Pub Date _____ Platform _____

Topic _____ Type _____

Hashtags/Keywords _____

Notes _____

_____

_____

_____

Post Pub Date _____ Platform _____

Topic _____ Type _____

Hashtags/Keywords _____

Notes _____

_____

_____

_____

Post Pub Date _____ Platform _____

Topic _____ Type _____

Hashtags/Keywords _____

Notes _____

_____

_____

_____

Post Pub Date _____ Platform _____

Topic _____ Type _____

Hashtags/Keywords _____

Notes _____

_____

_____

_____

---

Post Pub Date _____ Platform _____

Topic _____ Type _____

Hashtags/Keywords _____

Notes _____

_____

_____

_____

---

Post Pub Date _____ Platform _____

Topic _____ Type _____

Hashtags/Keywords _____

Notes _____

_____

_____

_____

---

Post Pub Date _____ Platform _____

Topic _____ Type _____

Hashtags/Keywords _____

Notes _____

_____

_____

_____

# Social Media Schedule

Week of _____

This Week's Focus _____

_____

| | Monday | Tuesday | Wednesday |
|---|---|---|---|
| Theme | | | |
| Platform & Post Time | | | |
| | | | |
| | | | |
| | | | |
| | | | |
| | | | |

| Thursday | Friday | Saturday | Sunday |
|----------|--------|----------|--------|
|          |        |          |        |
|          |        |          |        |
|          |        |          |        |
|          |        |          |        |
|          |        |          |        |
|          |        |          |        |

## Post Ideas Worksheet

Post Pub Date _____ Platform _____

Topic _____ Type _____

Hashtags/Keywords _____

Notes _____

_____

_____

Post Pub Date _____ Platform _____

Topic _____ Type _____

Hashtags/Keywords _____

Notes _____

_____

_____

Post Pub Date _____ Platform _____

Topic _____ Type _____

Hashtags/Keywords _____

Notes _____

_____

_____

Post Pub Date _____ Platform _____

Topic _____ Type _____

Hashtags/Keywords _____

Notes _____

_____

_____

Post Pub Date _____ Platform _____

Topic _____ Type _____

Hashtags/Keywords _____

Notes _____

_____

_____

Post Pub Date _____ Platform _____

Topic _____ Type _____

Hashtags/Keywords _____

Notes _____

_____

_____

Post Pub Date _____ Platform _____

Topic _____ Type _____

Hashtags/Keywords _____

Notes _____

_____

_____

Post Pub Date _____ Platform _____

Topic _____ Type _____

Hashtags/Keywords _____

Notes _____

_____

_____

# Social Media Schedule

Week of _____

This Week's Focus _____

_____

| | Monday | Tuesday | Wednesday |
|---|---|---|---|
| Theme | | | |
| Platform & Post Time | | | |
| | | | |
| | | | |
| | | | |
| | | | |
| | | | |

## Hashtags/Keywords

| Thursday | Friday | Saturday | Sunday |
|----------|--------|----------|--------|
|          |        |          |        |
|          |        |          |        |
|          |        |          |        |
|          |        |          |        |
|          |        |          |        |
|          |        |          |        |

## Post Ideas Worksheet

Post Pub Date _____ Platform _____

Topic _____ Type _____

Hashtags/Keywords _____

Notes _____

_____

_____

---

Post Pub Date _____ Platform _____

Topic _____ Type _____

Hashtags/Keywords _____

Notes _____

_____

_____

---

Post Pub Date _____ Platform _____

Topic _____ Type _____

Hashtags/Keywords _____

Notes _____

_____

_____

---

Post Pub Date _____ Platform _____

Topic _____ Type _____

Hashtags/Keywords _____

Notes _____

_____

_____

Post Pub Date _____ Platform _____

Topic _____ Type _____

Hashtags/Keywords _____

Notes _____

_____

_____

_____

---

Post Pub Date _____ Platform _____

Topic _____ Type _____

Hashtags/Keywords _____

Notes _____

_____

_____

_____

---

Post Pub Date _____ Platform _____

Topic _____ Type _____

Hashtags/Keywords _____

Notes _____

_____

_____

_____

---

Post Pub Date _____ Platform _____

Topic _____ Type _____

Hashtags/Keywords _____

Notes _____

_____

_____

_____

# Social Media Schedule

Week of _____

This Week's Focus _____

_____

| | Monday | Tuesday | Wednesday |
|---|---|---|---|
| Theme | | | |
| Platform & Post Time | | | |
| | | | |
| | | | |
| | | | |
| | | | |
| | | | |

Hashtags/Keywords _____

_____

_____

_____

| Thursday | Friday | Saturday | Sunday |
|----------|--------|----------|--------|
|          |        |          |        |
|          |        |          |        |
|          |        |          |        |
|          |        |          |        |
|          |        |          |        |
|          |        |          |        |

▶ Post Ideas Worksheet

Post Pub Date _____     Platform _____

Topic _____     Type _____

Hashtags/Keywords _____

Notes _____

_____

_____


Post Pub Date _____     Platform _____

Topic _____     Type _____

Hashtags/Keywords _____

Notes _____

_____

_____


Post Pub Date _____     Platform _____

Topic _____     Type _____

Hashtags/Keywords _____

Notes _____

_____

_____


Post Pub Date _____     Platform _____

Topic _____     Type _____

Hashtags/Keywords _____

Notes _____

_____

_____

Post Pub Date _____ Platform _____

Topic _____ Type _____

Hashtags/Keywords _____

Notes _____

_____

_____

_____

Post Pub Date _____ Platform _____

Topic _____ Type _____

Hashtags/Keywords _____

Notes _____

_____

_____

_____

Post Pub Date _____ Platform _____

Topic _____ Type _____

Hashtags/Keywords _____

Notes _____

_____

_____

_____

Post Pub Date _____ Platform _____

Topic _____ Type _____

Hashtags/Keywords _____

Notes _____

_____

_____

_____

# Social Media Schedule

Week of _____

This Week's Focus _____

_____

_____

| | Monday | Tuesday | Wednesday |
|---|---|---|---|
| Theme | | | |
| Platform & Post Time | | | |
| | | | |
| | | | |
| | | | |
| | | | |
| | | | |

| Thursday | Friday | Saturday | Sunday |
|----------|--------|----------|--------|
|          |        |          |        |
|          |        |          |        |
|          |        |          |        |
|          |        |          |        |
|          |        |          |        |
|          |        |          |        |

## Post Ideas Worksheet

Post Pub Date _____ Platform _____

Topic _____ Type _____

Hashtags/Keywords _____

Notes _____

_____

_____

Post Pub Date _____ Platform _____

Topic _____ Type _____

Hashtags/Keywords _____

Notes _____

_____

_____

Post Pub Date _____ Platform _____

Topic _____ Type _____

Hashtags/Keywords _____

Notes _____

_____

_____

Post Pub Date _____ Platform _____

Topic _____ Type _____

Hashtags/Keywords _____

Notes _____

_____

_____

Post Pub Date _____ Platform _____

Topic _____ Type _____

Hashtags/Keywords _____

Notes _____

_____

_____

_____

Post Pub Date _____ Platform _____

Topic _____ Type _____

Hashtags/Keywords _____

Notes _____

_____

_____

_____

Post Pub Date _____ Platform _____

Topic _____ Type _____

Hashtags/Keywords _____

Notes _____

_____

_____

_____

Post Pub Date _____ Platform _____

Topic _____ Type _____

Hashtags/Keywords _____

Notes _____

_____

_____

_____

## Social Media Schedule

Week of _____

This Week's Focus _____

_____

| | Monday | Tuesday | Wednesday |
|---|---|---|---|
| Theme | | | |
| Platform & Post Time | | | |
| | | | |
| | | | |
| | | | |
| | | | |
| | | | |

| Thursday | Friday | Saturday | Sunday |
|---|---|---|---|
|  |  |  |  |
|  |  |  |  |
|  |  |  |  |
|  |  |  |  |
|  |  |  |  |
|  |  |  |  |

## Post Ideas Worksheet

Post Pub Date _____ Platform _____

Topic _____ Type _____

Hashtags/Keywords _____

Notes _____

_____

_____

Post Pub Date _____ Platform _____

Topic _____ Type _____

Hashtags/Keywords _____

Notes _____

_____

_____

Post Pub Date _____ Platform _____

Topic _____ Type _____

Hashtags/Keywords _____

Notes _____

_____

_____

Post Pub Date _____ Platform _____

Topic _____ Type _____

Hashtags/Keywords _____

Notes _____

_____

_____

Post Pub Date _____ Platform _____

Topic _____ Type _____

Hashtags/Keywords _____

Notes _____

_____

_____

Post Pub Date _____ Platform _____

Topic _____ Type _____

Hashtags/Keywords _____

Notes _____

_____

_____

Post Pub Date _____ Platform _____

Topic _____ Type _____

Hashtags/Keywords _____

Notes _____

_____

_____

Post Pub Date _____ Platform _____

Topic _____ Type _____

Hashtags/Keywords _____

Notes _____

_____

_____

# Social Media Schedule

Week of _____

This Week's Focus _____

_____

|  | Monday | Tuesday | Wednesday |
|---|---|---|---|
| Theme |  |  |  |
| Platform & Post Time |  |  |  |
|  |  |  |  |
|  |  |  |  |
|  |  |  |  |
|  |  |  |  |

Hashtags/Keywords_____

_____

_____

| Thursday | Friday | Saturday | Sunday |
|----------|--------|----------|--------|
|          |        |          |        |
|          |        |          |        |
|          |        |          |        |
|          |        |          |        |
|          |        |          |        |
|          |        |          |        |

## Post Ideas Worksheet

Post Pub Date _____ Platform _____

Topic _____ Type _____

Hashtags/Keywords _____

Notes _____

_____

_____

Post Pub Date _____ Platform _____

Topic _____ Type _____

Hashtags/Keywords _____

Notes _____

_____

_____

Post Pub Date _____ Platform _____

Topic _____ Type _____

Hashtags/Keywords _____

Notes _____

_____

_____

Post Pub Date _____ Platform _____

Topic _____ Type _____

Hashtags/Keywords _____

Notes _____

_____

_____

Post Pub Date _____ Platform _____

Topic _____ Type _____

Hashtags/Keywords _____

Notes _____

_____

_____

_____

Post Pub Date _____ Platform _____

Topic _____ Type _____

Hashtags/Keywords _____

Notes _____

_____

_____

_____

Post Pub Date _____ Platform _____

Topic _____ Type _____

Hashtags/Keywords _____

Notes _____

_____

_____

_____

Post Pub Date _____ Platform _____

Topic _____ Type _____

Hashtags/Keywords _____

Notes _____

_____

_____

_____

# Social Media Schedule

Week of _____

This Week's Focus _____

_____

_____

| | Monday | Tuesday | Wednesday |
|---|---|---|---|
| Theme | | | |
| Platform & Post Time | | | |
| | | | |
| | | | |
| | | | |
| | | | |

| Thursday | Friday | Saturday | Sunday |
|----------|--------|----------|--------|
|          |        |          |        |
|          |        |          |        |
|          |        |          |        |
|          |        |          |        |
|          |        |          |        |
|          |        |          |        |

## Post Ideas Worksheet

Post Pub Date _____ Platform _____

Topic _____ Type _____

Hashtags/Keywords _____

Notes _____

_____

_____

Post Pub Date _____ Platform _____

Topic _____ Type _____

Hashtags/Keywords _____

Notes _____

_____

_____

Post Pub Date _____ Platform _____

Topic _____ Type _____

Hashtags/Keywords _____

Notes _____

_____

_____

Post Pub Date _____ Platform _____

Topic _____ Type _____

Hashtags/Keywords _____

Notes _____

_____

_____

Post Pub Date _____ Platform _____

Topic _____ Type _____

Hashtags/Keywords _____

Notes _____

_____

_____

_____

---

Post Pub Date _____ Platform _____

Topic _____ Type _____

Hashtags/Keywords _____

Notes _____

_____

_____

_____

---

Post Pub Date _____ Platform _____

Topic _____ Type _____

Hashtags/Keywords _____

Notes _____

_____

_____

_____

---

Post Pub Date _____ Platform _____

Topic _____ Type _____

Hashtags/Keywords _____

Notes _____

_____

_____

_____

# Social Media Schedule

Week of _____

This Week's Focus _____

_____

| | Monday | Tuesday | Wednesday |
|---|---|---|---|
| Theme | | | |
| Platform & Post Time | | | |
| | | | |
| | | | |
| | | | |
| | | | |
| | | | |

## Hashtags/Keywords

| Thursday | Friday | Saturday | Sunday |
|----------|--------|----------|--------|
|          |        |          |        |
|          |        |          |        |
|          |        |          |        |
|          |        |          |        |
|          |        |          |        |
|          |        |          |        |

Post Pub Date _____ Platform _____

Topic _____ Type _____

Hashtags/Keywords _____

Notes _____

_____

_____

Post Pub Date _____ Platform _____

Topic _____ Type _____

Hashtags/Keywords _____

Notes _____

_____

_____

Post Pub Date _____ Platform _____

Topic _____ Type _____

Hashtags/Keywords _____

Notes _____

_____

_____

Post Pub Date _____ Platform _____

Topic _____ Type _____

Hashtags/Keywords _____

Notes _____

_____

_____

Post Pub Date _____ Platform _____

Topic _____ Type _____

Hashtags/Keywords _____

Notes _____

_____

_____

---

Post Pub Date _____ Platform _____

Topic _____ Type _____

Hashtags/Keywords _____

Notes _____

_____

_____

---

Post Pub Date _____ Platform _____

Topic _____ Type _____

Hashtags/Keywords _____

Notes _____

_____

_____

---

Post Pub Date _____ Platform _____

Topic _____ Type _____

Hashtags/Keywords _____

Notes _____

_____

_____

# Social Media Schedule

Week of _____

This Week's Focus _____

_____

|  | Monday | Tuesday | Wednesday |
|---|---|---|---|
| Theme |  |  |  |
| Platform & Post Time |  |  |  |
|  |  |  |  |
|  |  |  |  |
|  |  |  |  |
|  |  |  |  |

## Hashtags/Keywords

| Thursday | Friday | Saturday | Sunday |
|----------|--------|----------|--------|
|          |        |          |        |
|          |        |          |        |
|          |        |          |        |
|          |        |          |        |
|          |        |          |        |
|          |        |          |        |

## ▶ Post Ideas Worksheet

Post Pub Date _____ Platform _____

Topic _____ Type _____

Hashtags/Keywords _____

Notes _____

_____

_____

---

Post Pub Date _____ Platform _____

Topic _____ Type _____

Hashtags/Keywords _____

Notes _____

_____

_____

---

Post Pub Date _____ Platform _____

Topic _____ Type _____

Hashtags/Keywords _____

Notes _____

_____

_____

---

Post Pub Date _____ Platform _____

Topic _____ Type _____

Hashtags/Keywords _____

Notes _____

_____

_____

Post Pub Date _____ Platform _____

Topic _____ Type _____

Hashtags/Keywords _____

Notes _____

_____

_____

Post Pub Date _____ Platform _____

Topic _____ Type _____

Hashtags/Keywords _____

Notes _____

_____

_____

Post Pub Date _____ Platform _____

Topic _____ Type _____

Hashtags/Keywords _____

Notes _____

_____

_____

Post Pub Date _____ Platform _____

Topic _____ Type _____

Hashtags/Keywords _____

Notes _____

_____

_____

Social Media Schedule

Week of _____

This Week's Focus _____

_____

|  | Monday | Tuesday | Wednesday |
|---|---|---|---|
| Theme | | | |
| Platform & Post Time | | | |
| | | | |
| | | | |
| | | | |
| | | | |
| | | | |

| Thursday | Friday | Saturday | Sunday |
|----------|--------|----------|--------|
|          |        |          |        |
|          |        |          |        |
|          |        |          |        |
|          |        |          |        |
|          |        |          |        |
|          |        |          |        |

Printed in Great Britain
by Amazon

56833616R00068